S0-AHM-367

MiCHAEL
SHOWS OFF BALTIMORE

ILLUSTRATED BY ART SEIDEN

Text provided by the Fifth Grade Class
Friends School, Baltimore

Tour leader: Michael, a Scottish Terrier

OUTDOOR BOOKS, NATURE SERIES, INC. BALTIMORE, MARYLAND

Copyright © 1982 Outdoor Books, Nature Series, Inc. Baltimore, Maryland 21218 ISBN 0-942806-01-8

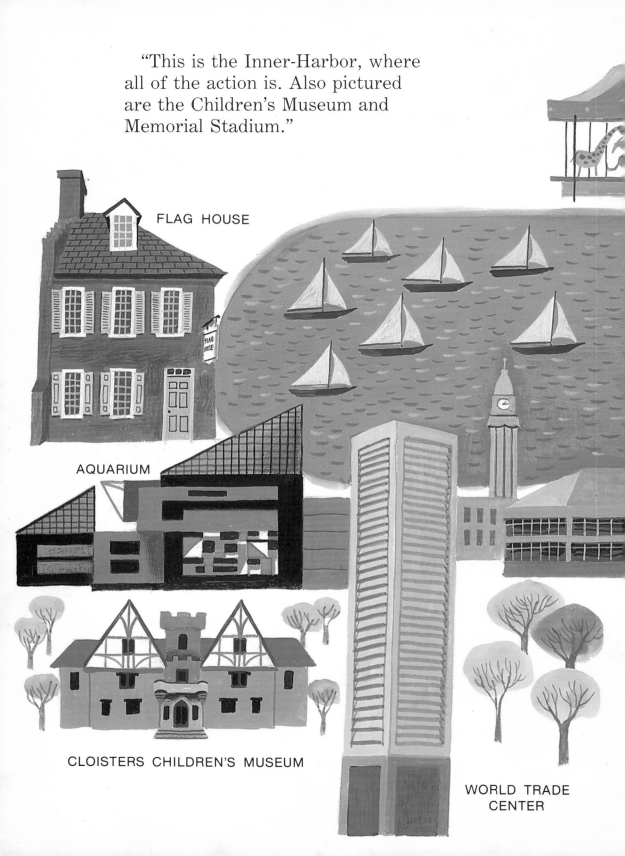

"This is the Inner-Harbor, where all of the action is. Also pictured are the Children's Museum and Memorial Stadium."

FLAG HOUSE

AQUARIUM

CLOISTERS CHILDREN'S MUSEUM

WORLD TRADE CENTER

MARYLAND SCIENCE MUSEUM

HARBOR PLACE

MEMORIAL STADIUM

"When you first walk into the National Aquarium there are sea lions."

"The Children's Cove has crabs, sea horses,
and shells you can pick up and hold."

"At the Maryland Science Center you can
learn about the metric system. They also have a
lot of experiments you can try. I like the video games."

"Down below the deck on the submarine Torsk,
you can go into the captains cabin, and look into
the periscope."

"The USS Constellation gives you a good feel
of history because, now, when you think of
ships, you think of big destroyers and things
that have so much electric equipment. It is a
good place to go because, if you look at it inside,
you can tell what conditions sailors lived in long ago."

"There are so many different kinds of animals at the Baltimore zoo. Of course, I am not allowed to visit there, but you may take your tour while I wait for you outside."

"Francis Scott Key wrote our National
Anthem about a battle that was fought at
Fort McHenry. They fly a big flag over the
Fort, and they show a movie about the battle."

"At the Baltimore Museum of Art there is one guy sitting there thinking. I wonder what he is thinking?"

"There are doll exhibits at the Cloisters Children's Museum. My little sister likes the doll house."

"At the Baltimore and Ohio Railroad Museum there is a model of Tom Thumb, one of the first train engines. Tom Thumb once raced a horse, and you can see them race."

"TOM THUMB"

"In the lower level
at the Walters Gallery
of Art, in a place that
looks like a dungeon,
they have armor from
all over."

"What I like about the Babe Ruth House is the big chart about all of the balls he hit, and all the different games he played in."

"At the Flag House, they show how flags were made a long time ago, including the Star Spangled Banner, which was made there."

"The Baltimore Colts and the Baltimore Orioles play their games at Memorial Stadium."

"At Fells Point you can see big ships and lots of colorful tug boats. Fells Point also has art galleries and tiny old houses."

"Baltimore has festivals all summer long celebrating the different people who live in the city. I like the Irish Festival. On the Fourth of July they shoot off fireworks from a boat in the harbor, and in the fall there is a big city fair."